Breakfast

Contents

Breakfast

This family is having breakfast.
What are they eating?

milk

eggs

bread

corn flakes

orange juice

Where does this food come from?

Where does milk come from?

1 Milk comes from cows.

2 Farmers milk the cows.

3 The milk goes to a factory.

4 The milk is put into cartons.

Where do eggs come from?

1 Eggs come from chickens.
Chickens lay eggs.

2 The eggs go to a factory.

3 The eggs are put into cartons.

Where does bread come from?

1 Bread is made from wheat. Farmers grow wheat. The wheat is cut.

2 The wheat goes to a mill. It is turned into flour.

3 The flour is made into bread.

Where do corn flakes come from?

1 Corn flakes come from corn. Farmers grow corn.

2 The corn is cut.

3 The corn goes to a factory.

4 The corn is
turned into
corn flakes.

Where does orange juice come from?

1 Oranges grow on trees.

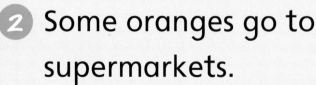

2 Some oranges go to supermarkets.

2 Some oranges go to factories. They are squeezed to make juice.

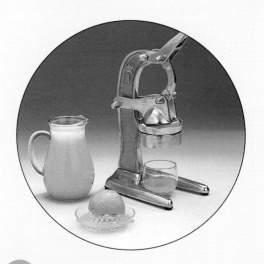

3 The oranges are squeezed by hand.

3 The orange juice is put into cartons.

Breakfast chart

Milk

Eggs

Bread

Corn flakes

Orange juice

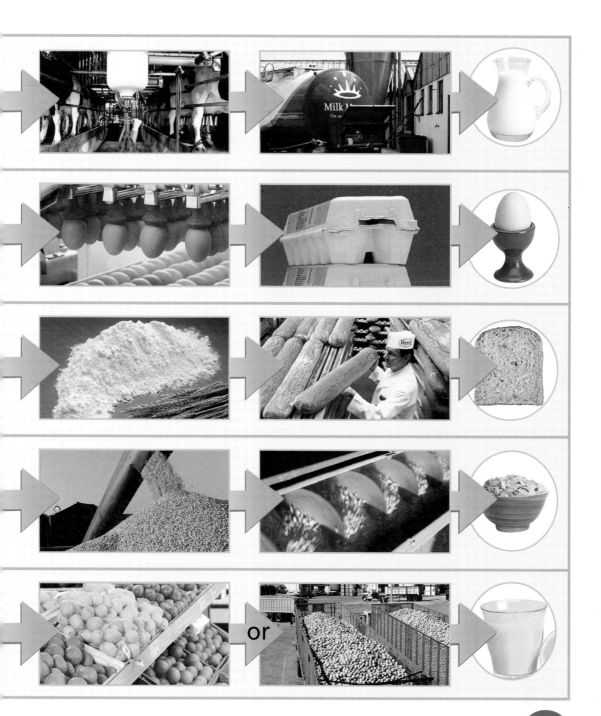

or

Index